BLEEDING RAINBOWS
A N D
OTHER BROKEN SPECTRUMS

MAXWELL I. GOLD

PRAISE

"With this bold collection of desiccated erotic fantasies, Maxwell I. Gold creates a dread-palace of beautiful perversion. Confronting and brimming with universal truth, Bleeding Rainbows is a primal and dangerous work. Authentic and affective."

—**Lee Murray**, four-time Bram Stoker Award®-winning author of *Grotesque: Monster Stories*

"A bold, visceral collection that pushes past comfort zones into a fever dream of raw, ugly truths refracted by the spinning disco ball of Gold's audacious poetic storytelling. Anchored in tremendous humanity, *Bleeding Rainbows and Other Broken Spectrums* will transport readers through their own personal infernos of guilt, shame, and utter imperfection, shooting them out somewhere into a cosmic void where voracious mirror monsters are slain by the healing light of self-forgiveness."

—**Vince A. Liaguno**, Bram Stoker Award®-winning editor of *Unspeakable Horror: From the Shadows of the Closet and Other Terrors: An Inclusive Anthology*

"If Zeus picked up Ganymede in a gay bathhouse, if Laura met Carmilla in a BDSM dungeon for vampires, their tales of supernatural sexual awakening would resemble the poetry in Maxwell Gold's terrifying—and incredibly sexy—*Bleeding Rainbows and Other Broken Spectrums*. Gay sex isn't relegated to metaphor in Gold's steamy verse, for *Bleeding Rainbows* has smashed all of its closets, freeing the monsters who live within and shining its fearless light on the many ways in which they arouse us. Vampires, werewolves, and the ancient gods themselves are as hungry as they are mesmerizing, and are prowling your local nightclub where they dangerously exude the seductive aroma of leather."

—**Sumiko Saulson**, Bram Stoker Award®-nominated author of *The Rat King, A Book of Dark Poetry*

"Maxwell I. Gold's poetry is a Hadron Collider for the imagination, smashing raw fantasy into visceral reality to create a poetic God particle—a dark deity of cosmic horror and wonder, as uncompromising as it is unexpected. If one's body really is a temple, then prepare for the dark deity to repaint your interior with every shade of sensual ruin and chaotic survival in the Bleeding Rainbow. And rejoice."
—**John Edward Lawson**, author of *Bibliophobia*

"*Bleeding Rainbows* is an intimate exploration of the cosmic and the erotic that jumps off the page with divine pleasures readers are sure to savor. This collection brings to mind Clive Barker's work, and like Barker, Gold presents a dark, interstellar read filled with the promise of forbidden yet deeply sought-after rapture."
—**Stephanie M. Wytovich**, Bram Stoker Award®-winning author of *Brothel*

BLEEDING RAINBOWS

RAINBOWS

AND

OTHER BROKEN
SPECTRUMS

MAXWELL I. GOLD

HEX PUBLISHERS

BLEEDING RAINBOWS
AND OTHER BROKEN SPECTRUMS

Illustrations by Martini
Art direction by Joshua Viola
Copyedits by Carina Bissett, Bret Smith, and Jeanni Smith
Cover by Damonza.com and Joshua Viola
Typesets and formatting by Alec Ferrell

A Hex Publishers Book

Published & Distributed by Hex Publishers, LLC
PO BOX 298
Erie, CO 80516

www.HexPublishers.com

Joshua Viola, Publisher

Hardcover ISBN: 979-8-9862194-9-3
Paperback ISBN: 978-1-7365964-4-9
e-Book ISBN: 978-1-7365964-5-6

First Edition: June 2023
10 9 8 7 6 5 4 3 2 1

Printed in the U.S.A.

CONTENTS

INTRODUCTION
ANGELA YURIKO SMITH

WARNING: this book will cut you.

I discovered this firsthand. I wasn't expecting Maxwell's collection to dredge up monsters I thought I'd smothered long ago. His poetry filled their sagging lungs, giving new buoyancy to old hurts. As I read, my personal demons surfaced one by one, fetid, rotting memories rolling on the surface of my conscious mind. My own humiliations, abuses, longings... like responded to like. This collection gave me nightmares. This collection is doing its job.

I know Maxwell as a friend, a co-author and a colleague. We first met when he started a conversation with me about his submission to *Space & Time* magazine. He wasn't interested in hearing how wonderful his work was. He contacted me to ask how his story, already good, could be better. As long as I've known him, he is always striving to push himself beyond his limitations.

"I learned that courage was not the absence of fear, but the triumph over it." Whenever I read this quote from Nelson Mandela I think of Max. He isn't the boldest person you will ever meet, but in spite of his quiet nature he has always stepped up to new challenges. I am constantly inspired by the way he confronts every challenge, not only in life but in his work. He confronts every obstacle he comes across without any bullshit posturing. As both a friend and a colleague, I've come to think of Maxwell as someone willing to push boundaries, but never leave anyone behind. He is one of the kindest people I know.

I also know better than to expect safe poetry from Maxwell. He isn't afraid to pull the mask off of his fear. He isn't squeamish when it comes to bloodletting. If you meet him in person he will come off as a quiet, friendly person, but don't be fooled. I would trust him with my life, but when it comes to pouring mayhem and nightmares onto paper, he's a fiend. Still, the raw intensity of this collection floored me.

It's this willingness to scream into the cosmic void that makes me love Maxwell both as an artist and a person. He isn't a "bro-god" here to prove anything to anyone, but in this collection, he shows his true badass core. It's easy to swagger, but to allow your vulnerabilities to be exposed is true guts. He not only bares everything (along with the incredible art pieces by Martini), but he also builds. Maxwell takes the raw shreds of sinew and broken bone from his past and creates a bridge of empathy—the pain connects us.

This poetry is gay, but you don't have to be gay to be affected by it. It resonates with anyone able to experience emotion. Who among us hasn't wept in utter rejection, who can claim to have never been shattered by loss? Whether we have been the victim or the abuser—or both—we can read our own histories here in this collection. See for yourself.

In "Night Club-ed Dreams" Maxwell captures the ego-crushing debasement that is the club scene for many of us with the first line:

Fire, funk, and empty treasons carried me through the flesh-throngs...

All the despair, false hope, and tragedy inherent in a superficial party life is packed into *Crimson Lips*, the first of seven sections.

A strong beginning, but also personally my favorite section because it brings back that time in my own life. From *Crimson Lips*, Maxwell embarks on a technicolor odyssey through his personal infernos.

In spite of the painful and ugly topics, Maxwell brings a beauty to them. Not glorifying the negative, but insisting on a recognition that we are not perfect beings, and never will be. But in spite of our limitations, perhaps even because of them, we are beautiful.

He speaks to the intangible, impermanent bags of flesh and bone we are, and reminds us that somehow we each contain fragments of star seed within us. He confesses himself to be a broken miracle. He encourages by his confessions.

But to hold weight, a confession must be honest. This isn't a finger-wagging volume of pontification. There is a foundation of candor throughout. Maxwell admits his fallibility. He is so upfront that in some ways he victimizes himself, a distinctly human trait. From "Oblivion's Bedroom:"

...if I wasn't already doomed, it didn't matter, the needle-like euphoria which emblazoned what was left of my perceived sense beautified my decayed conscious...

Like bitter tonic, the words burn as we swallow them, but they reveal and heal. From "Stonewalled / Sing for Myself:"

> *We held the songs of the universe,*
> *Composed in flesh and star-boned nights...*

Decay, shame, self-loathing, loss... It sounds demoralizing but this is no Morrissey-flavored rant of self-pity. Maxwell I. Gold has brought to these pages vivid truth and empathy. By sharing his own pain and struggle, he passes on strength to the rest of us.

From "When Rainbows Bleed," he leaves a promise:

No more dark jubilations,
but Uranian joy everlasting...

Dealing with topics of physical and mental abuse, this is not a volume of quick and easy poetry. This is the book you need to read at midnight during the worst night of your life, and then again when you've won the next morning. This is a book you give to a co-worker you suspect might need the medicine. This book is the friend that will hold your hair back while you throw up your regrets. These words are from someone who has been there and has the scars to show it.

The truth isn't pretty, but somehow Maxwell captures the flaws and fractures we all try to hide. He holds them up to the frenetic strobe of his past and casts forth rainbows from broken glass. In this light, we all look different. We look like ourselves.

This is not just a collection about Pride. This is a manual for survival. This should be required reading on relationships. It's a treatise on toxic masculinity. It's a cautionary tale, but more than all of that, it's a raw and powerful look at cosmic darkness, the universe within and the light that waits for all of us just beyond the event horizon.

Crimson Lips

Take My Hand,
And I'll Carry You Onward;
Take My Hand.

The First Triangle

Marks like memory bruised my body each night when I saw those hands. Three times, three familiar whips across my skin were the voices which called from the past: bloodied, broken, and imbued by pink daggers wrought from shadows that stalked my—no our—history like hungry gods. We were the chimney babes too, condemned for love, sex, and existence then crucified on brick and bone as if to frighten the spirit of lust from our bodies.

How often I wandered streets where every door was a closet and windows were triangles, but through each gateway the same hand, outstretched and willing, presented itself from behind a curtain of death and shadow.

Take my hand, the voice said.

Emblazoned across his palm, marks like memory bruised his body when each night I dreamed he'd pull me from a world that sought my destruction, past his curtain of stars.

Erased

I lost myself in him,
With him, through every touch
and terrible possibility
that came with the darkness;

I lost everything the moment
His eyes corrupted caught me,
Like some sweet drink,
or blood-mixed in metal
as if I was a zombified fucktoy,
Controlled and twisted;

I lost everything
On the other side of the curtain,
Drunk on stars and sin
And eyes so terrible
They meant everything and nothing;

I lost my body, destroyed
Myself in a bed that became my grave
Alone in a palace of night, dagger and
Betrayal was the only thing I knew;

I lost everyone who said I was mad
When I stepped into the arms of a god
That promised me the universe
And delivered my worst fears,
Erased by both unimaginable pleasure and fear;

I lost myself in him,
with him, through every touch
and terrible possibility.

Monster in the Closet

He was hideous, and I couldn't take my eyes off him. Covered in strands of wiry, vascular grotesqueness, I capitulated at the feet of a flesh-monolith who lumbered in the dim, dark stars of an unforgiving age. Through temples built of sweat, metal, and leather I stalked him, a beast of my own construction whose form in muscle and death with baritone laughter spilled across the floor of that pantheon of closets and curses, as if I were nothing but a crumb beneath him. God, he was dreadfully beautiful, and I'd never be able to have him, never as I was or as the world saw me.

Collapsed beneath the weight of expectations and doors that shut without reason, I lusted for the monstrosity who mocked me and never saw the truth, the light that was me. He was hideous, and I couldn't take my eyes off that monster.

Night Club-ed Dreams

Fire, funk, and empty treasons carried me through the flesh-throngs where I found myself hot, heavy, and trapped beneath the familiar stink and song of a grand burlesque-ed temple. Monsters, Jock-Queens, and Rainbow Gods danced in this disco-dungeon lost in cosmic gyrations, tossed away like some plaything to my own primal urges, as songs blared and bodies danced to familiar rituals.

A red-faced man, or monster, like a shadow stood over me though I was not to be sure, but he slid through the mass of glossy-eyed, wonderous debauchery, luring my countenance past spectral gardens beneath pounding stars towards the edge of the temple.

Take my hand, he spoke with a soothing, bass-like utterance where then a triangle so bright, beckoned for my touch as if I had waited for a thousand awful years to grasp it. Too late was I when, past the curtain of stars, he took me to twist my mind with possibilities I never dared to conceive but had always wished to see.

Swipe to the...

Psychosexual heartbeats, wrapped inside computerized sensations, were the drumbeats of the future. The new wave of love, lust, and never-ending search for the faceless, unforgiving familiars threw me against a wall in pleasurable nightmarish desire; liars behind a screen, liars with phantom smiles and false bodies of muscle and mania were nothing but erotic ghouls who swiped right behind me.

Another liar, another heartbeat concealed in sweat, bytes, and jock-tissue consumed my blood-red desire until I was brought to the highest point of climax where the horizon pressed against the wide, starry birth of my sensory universe until the inevitable collapse. Drawn down by the raucous laughter of phantom smiles who wanted nothing more than to gut and hollow out everything that remained, everything I knew to be true.

God, it wasn't enough.

To the right,

To the left,

Where another faceless promise stared from behind the walls of my cyber prison only to reveal another cycle to repeat, more heartbeats to throb and burn from inside and out.

To the left,

To the right,

Until the cycle repeated, endlessness, and I was wrapped forever inside computerized sensations of psychosexual pleasure.

Eros, My Eros

Two souls, three heads, five hearts,
desires knew not a boundary, marker, nor design like flesh,
only the missing piece be it a kiss, lovesick scar, or ruined
heart twisted by the make-believe thoughts and constructs
by a world that was never meant to hold us apart;
confined to chambers full to the brim with blood-soaked yearning
where the meter ticks ever higher until the soft touch of flesh
and fire combine in radiant, destructive beauty
to unite that which was pulled apart like the stars themselves
torn asunder by Gravity's hideous intensity.
Two souls, three heads, five hearts,
one muscle, desire knew not
my heavy love for Eros, my Eros.

My Crimson Lips

Wandering through gray storms of ice, rock, and glass where dead castles and wild Rimbaudian palaces stretched into the cold, libidinous night, I swallowed deep pangs of a never-ending, desiccating thirst. My lips were soaked, bubbling with liquescent crimson pleasure, drops of ecstasy splashing onto my skin, the bloated, fetid corpse at my feet, drained entirely of blood and beauty. They were the last ones, the last vessels in a cold, lifeless tower, as my hunger only grew worse throbbing with an insatiable wanting. The air was soaked with a thick intoxicating scent of rust, sweat, and leather as I stalked the halls, the ancient moon grinning through a marble aperture, appalled by my grotesque, sensual appetites.

More! I cried, my fingers twisted, popped, and cracked in immense undulating pleasure, caressing the pile of decayed flesh and ligaments, seeking to quench that thirst, which was monstrous and unbearable, like a deep chasm with a beast lurking in the unimaginable bottom. Soon, the hideous moon reached its awful zenith in the night where all at once, I was lost in a furious rage of bloody sanguinity, chewing, gnashing, and singing wildly into the frozen Voids. "More! There has to be more!" I cried, the moon winking from its perch, mocking me in the firmaments as I started, pulling, tearing, and licking the moist, fleshy carcass. Calcite daggers dragged across the surface, pleading sensually for one more drop. My lips were soaked, bubbling with pleasure, the soft drops exploding onto my skin, the bloated, fêted corpse at my feet, drained entirely of blood and beauty.

My Crown, My Top

Red crowns atop a castle of thorns so sharp, deadly, and dark pierced my soul, yet I couldn't help myself from his rubescent glare. So tall, each barb pushed with scrutinizingly intense joy into my skin. A laugh here, a kiss there; once more I passed through the gate, inside him.

Past the crimson curtain where I was shown the wonder of stars and light, I cared not about pathetic bodily quivers or tremulous sensations, only wild ululations emanating from that most precious spark when his eyes met mine.

Over and over, teeth scraped o'er my tired brain wishing to wear that bejeweled, cursed top, wishing him to crush me under such unbearable weight as he had done so many nights before in chambers sealed, never spoken, locked inside his castle of red crowns.

Take My Hand

Take my hand, said the flesh-god of red desire whose body stood
at the curtain of my nightmarish thirst, his words the last
thing I heard before any sense I had was completely paralyzed
under the guise of burning eyes who;

Take my hand with each flash and fragrant wave, behind the white
mask which concealed far more than a chiseled face, or sly grin,
but the dark unreasonable desire pleading to;

Take my hand beyond the responsibility of the present, bathing
me in the unwashed liquescence of fornicated dreams where my
fantasies were made real, the past a lifeless corpse and his
outstretched fingers;

Take my hand through the curtain of stars into the tubes of
deep-down twilight, this nameless man who knew nothing of my
truths except the billowing blood-plumes in my soul, each one
like some awful throb, one after the other;

Take my hand, though I couldn't help but resist the darkness
beyond and the awful possibilities, said the flesh-god who
finally got everything he wanted when he took my hand.

Through the Curtain Once More

It began underneath the cream-cloud bedsheets that I saw sparkling fantasies, new dreads, composed with stale odors and bleached sensations that dragged me closer to the breach. Red hands, long fingers pulled back the sheets, slowly, deliberately. I'd been here before, so warm and welcoming as if the crimson flesh were like that of an old friend, or a lover from centuries past longing to embrace me once more.

I knew those hands, echoes of a terrible past. Open palm drew towards the vast stars where vein and vaulted nights twitched underneath the burning stars, whose lust for entropy and energy bubbled as the towering figure pulled me deeper, through the curtains once more.

Bacterial Desires

Down,
     Down,
          Through the depths, the wraiths
wailed, dancing in funk and foul fantasy;
     come with me.
Down,
     Down,
          Into the swamps where everything
          is hidden,

          I am your bacterial desire...

The Second Triangle

Marks followed, changed, evolved like the rest of us, burning throughout the aeons, swallowed inside falsified truths of what was or wasn't and so;

Marks followed us everywhere, desire crawled towards perversion where love bled into fetish and nowhere within the planes of flesh or thought;

Marks continued to move, change, and hunt, transmogrified by the worst and most fantastic inhibitions of ourselves into something both unrecognizable and beautiful. Until we were changed, evolved, proud of the marks that were entirely ours.

My Worst Nightmare

I was in love with the most beautiful nightmare, conceived in the blackest, most awful place, a gaslit madhouse of my own demented thoughts. Fingers, crooked and dim, rose from the floor, dancing across my eyes, pulling me towards the fucked-phallacies that soaked my brain in syrupy desires where the putrid, fleshy digits tugged, clawed, and carried me away.

Begging me to lie with them in a bed composed of desiccated fantasy, too sexed up to see what was on the other end, underneath the bed. On the other side of my nightmares, something dark, muddied, but that didn't matter because I was in love with my worst nightmare.

A Second Variation

It was hard to see through the fog of such intense hatred. Objectified pluralities forged in baneful constructs soon became my world. It wasn't a real place but, wrapped within the cloth and cult of his touch, it felt like the only place that mattered. A grotesque wonderland personified by *his* truth where reason deafened under screams and scars, all suffocated by the scent of bleach and stale paint.

I'd been here before.

Somehow, I thought I'd escape this dread-palace where monsters were preferred and brain matter curdled into ash, though it felt as if nothing existed before I came here, before *he* came and consumed everything. The murk was thick, filled with a dank familiarity. Sharp pangs rushed through my chest as if a heavy stone pressed against my heart.

It must be a trick, and I had to get out.

Inside his trash-castle, where towers of drywall, paint, and blood coated every ounce of my visceral experiences, I was the object, helpless and fragile, drawing ever closer despite not being able to see *him*. I knew he was coming. The imperious trembling of each footfall as my body involuntarily convulsed behind the door, of course that was how he wanted it.

Fuck. Not this time.

I knew it was hard to see, to understand when confined behind the high walls of a selfish, black hatred; I'd never let him have his way...Never again.

Rêves Érotiques: Ancient Desires

I.
Of Unwilling Gods and Silence

Longing, waiting, heaving under the smoothness of a heavy exegetical silence, shadows throbbed between the fingers of gods. The tremendous undulations of their bodies, rocking in hot bedchambers consigned to some protean-fetishized hell, raged with an unforeseen Hadean desire, hungrily groping the night. Their fingers, composed from the ashy dust and crag of broken worlds, trembled with a thousand eroticisms, where one thousand more planets quaked as the Gods of Feast and Fuck lay hungry, encumbered by liquid blackness covering their bodies. Limbs and lips prepared to swallow what remained of the dark, tattered and tired and unable to dance, bestrode by hungering eyes. Longing, waiting, heaving under the smoothness of a heavy exegetical silence, shadows throbbed between the fingers of gods, an unwilling fornication by titans and beasts.

II.
Bacterial Desires

Mitochondrial urges, genetic pleasures writhing with rhythm and rocking against the backdrop of a billion carnal voices, grew in the fleshy peripherals of time. Faster and louder, it seemed unstoppable, this ancient sensation drenched in guttural pleasures, moaning with erotic blasphemies as stars made love with daemons in the dark.

Past empty voids of molten dreams, where rotting nightmares shed their skins of dissonant dread, only to reveal a dank cocoon of silvery platitudes; only then did the sweet music grow. Blasting pleasurable melodies, one after the other, until the immense galactic mass spilled over our pitiful existence whose vulnerabilities were laid bare at its feet, helpless and pure. And so, it would continue, these cosmic desires forged in our darkest bedchambers and etched into a primal consciousness without heed, acting on instinct and lust.

Mitochondrial urges, genetic pleasures writing with rhythm and rocking against the backdrop of a billion carnal voices, grew in the fleshy peripherals of time. One after the other, showers of stardust curdled the sheets of spacetime, staining the innocence of reality.

III.
Languor

When all was silent, gods no longer hungered for flesh or music. Hedonistic palettes emptied, barren and bleached, stripped of their galactic thirsts, leaving only dimness and dull, contrite fantasies. Though, towards the desolate edges of dreamy lustful platitudes, one pitiful creature sought the final embrace of entropic sanguinity, one last drop. Floating through the emptiness of an uncaring and carnal universe, this piece of existence, while forgotten to dying gods and planets, drew ever closer towards swirling infinities, wrapped in nuclear ecstasy. Writhing and twisting, one pitiful creature found only languor, and the dreaminess of a thousand unsung songs when all was silent, gods no longer hungered for flesh or music.

IV.
Machinations

Beat, fuck, throb, repeat. Stars blinking, voids in the dark. Beat, fuck, throb, repeat. Stars emptied, drained from sacs of bacterial nothingness. Binary signals locked in blood, those evolutionary cravings, piles, heat, sensations repeated over countless billions of years. Growing musty, under the salty liquescent moonlight, primal and dangerous, while starquakes trembled, blasting foamy white stardust from some Promethean orifices in the night. Beat, fuck, throb, repeat. Stars blinking, voids in the dark. Beat, fuck, throb, repeat. Stars emptied, drained from sacs of bacterial nothingness.

V.
Bytes and Bruises: A Fetish Called Reality

Within the vacuous cyber dark, neon wraiths piled onto each other, tangled in cloaks of simulated fucks, bytes, and bruises. Circulated vessels emptied of flesh replicating an orgasmic theory, throngs of metallic things, these inhuman cyber deviants danced in streets of plastic and parables to the sounds of scratching, gnawing, and writhing, hoping to taste, or even smell something so sweet. Organic truths were lost in this place of robotic, bestial urges, and sexual bodies transcending a fleshy subsistence. Harder, pressed under cold, compressed fingers groping cloaks of code and calculus, transgressive projections wailed with an atomic ecstasy. Within the vacuous cyber dark, neon wraiths piled onto each other, tangled in cloaks of simulated fucks, bytes, and bruises.

VI.
Cyber Fuckery

Stringy dreams, floating within my silky thoughts, played like clockwork along broken synapses and a foggy consciousness. Hypnotized by the dance of a thousand faceless drones whirling in my head, I saw shadows and silhouettes writhe in the night teasing my hungry primordia, throbbing deep inside a twisted god. My mind quickly devolved into nothing less than a crazed delirious mess, where laughing gods and silver whores thrashed about in some plane of existence of liquescent shadows pressing against foggy mirrors, as their rusty lips kissed me with their oxidized, bloody smell. Everything was without reason or symmetry, without melody or cognizance.

All the while, pangs of bright light and dissonant groans, groped the brain-tissue of my mind, tossing me back to the beginning, to the place where it all began. A place where longing, waiting, heaving under the smoothness of a heavy exegetical silence, shadows throbbed between the fingers of gods, an unwilling fornication by titans and beasts wrapped inside stringy dreams floating within my silky white nightmares.

Eight Billion Desires

Drained by monstrous expectations, prudent and artificial structures by which my true dreams were suppressed into rotting, shameful pits, I was forced to make a choice. Deeper, longer, and after every day confined to my abyssal prison, I found myself like the rest of the world, tired of skulking along the peripherals of so many indifferent eyes—Eyes which never knew the carnal desire locked inside me. Those unspoken treasures, and bloated Dionysian fantasies painted the ravaged cathedrals and sanctuaries of my nightmares with lurid, erotic Uranian truths.

No longer contained by the despicable roots of cold eyes or metal systems, I rose from the pit. Naked and filled with blood and star-boned jubilance, I stood over a city in flames where thousands gawked, fled, and even kneeled in my shadow. My lips parted, happily taken as the object of their darkest fears and desires; I beckoned. *Take nothing...* Higher I went still, the city bestrode by my immensity covered in lust and ruin; I knew it was finished. *...for I am your desire.*

Cyanide Surprises

i.

Pop one, kiss two,
It'll only hurt a little, he said.
Crack, snap, another star dead —
Another piece lost —
Another piece of myself,

Lost in the game,
The endless beauty-muck.

Fuck one, kiss three,
The pain goes away.
Crack, push, no more,
No more stars,
No more pieces to lose,
No more pieces left

Only cyanide surprises,
Lost in the game,
Drowned in the beauty-muck;

ii.

Down the rabbit hole,
where the veins opened like some phantasmic tubular dream-
cruise. Fill the Void, more pressure, forget the pain until the
stars and screams subsided, the wild claxon wailing like inane
trumpets the only reasonable music that played in my bruised
brain as I hungered for

one

    more

        pop,

                                      one

                                  more

                              kiss;

iii.

From the Void was all I needed;
It'll only hurt a little, he lied.
Crack, push, snap,
No more pieces to lose,
No more pieces to give.

He Had Everything,
In the Eye of the City

Where oblivions trembled beneath black nights, a nameless city, familiar and strange to me, beheld the erotic, terrifying truth which cracked inside my brain. A revelation no more, my head turned towards flesh-pillars coiled around the sky, afraid to call them what they truly were, trapped within the confines of his reality. Wandering those streets, covered in ice, blood, and bone, I saw immense structures cleaved from light and dust, reflecting alien auroras across a darkened sky.

Blink.

Throb.

Blink. Repeat.

The unbearable chill of the air wrought terrible sensations of paresthesia throughout my body, as I continued down the empty snow-covered streets, my only comfort, the howling winds and laughter like a baritone chuckle slapping my back.

Blink.

Throb.

Blink. Repeat.

Another flesh toy for him to use, abuse, and collect. Soon, his laughter grew in awful crescendo, my ears bleeding as flesh-fingered towers rocked the city with metallic symphonies rupturing the artificial atmosphere. Even the magnificent auroras slowly crumbled, atom by atom, into nothing but pitiful quantum shells.

Don't look up, were the tired, useless utterances in my head, weakened by dark, heavy objectification and thrown about as if in the hands of some evil god.

Blink.
  Throb.
    Blink. Repeat.

I couldn't help myself. The urge was too much, and the temptation infinitely strong when suddenly a profound and great calamity pressed its weight over the beleaguered city, and me. Walls of flesh, muscle, and metal stretched beyond the stars, as the mass of fingers compressed over the city.

Blink.
  Throb.
    Blink. Repeat.

Ruptured was my soul, staring into the perfidious reflection of myself, deformed and monstrous; while wandering the streets, covered in ice, blood, and bone, I saw immense structures of light and dust; where frozen oblivions trembled underneath black vacuous nights, and a nameless city was trapped within the metal confines of my jagged, geometrical reality.

Second Thoughts

They told me he was everything; how could you leave? Get out from his awful clutches, coarse manipulations, and twisted kisses. This wasn't about *them*. Nothing is ever what it seems, though through the rose-colored nights and cheap, blended colognes, I felt the warmth of someday caress the welts on my shoulders, black eyes, and bruised dreams of self-worth. Sweetly, words slowly corroded into broken promises and hallucinatory denials where *us* morphed *into* him, and everything existed inside *his world.* An abominable universe bleached by untruths and a screened-in porch where reality was beyond my reach. Ripped carpets where rusty nails jutted out from rickety floorboards and every other awful night pain was inevitable, and his gentle fingers down my back grew into shiners which were never meant to be; though simply cooed accident to those who thought they knew better. *He'd never actually hurt you,* they told me.

He was such a bastard...and the planets cried, tears of remorseless fire and stardust where, within the bastard's prideful darkness, he dragged me across rusty nails and broken floorboards.
It's only a scratch; bile oozed from crinkled lips with tool and rancor, a heavy odor of smoke and lies filled the air. I had to get out, no matter even if the universe imploded, or if oblivion came to us both. *It's only a scratch*, the last few times he said as quiet screams in the night were muffled by cotton and coddled under the soft glow of the moon when I finally left that place.

Turbellarian Dreams

The sky was full of worms and rot, and the last bits of my useless mania fell from the shattered corpses of Binary Monsters. Holes and hungry silos like puckered lips, kissed the erogenous chunk of night, over and over until no more did the monsters threaten our existence. Caught between primal transformations and artificial banalities, I felt the walls of flesh press harder over the heavy skies where holes closed deeper around the felled beast.

Monstrous and created with the need to compartmentalize my desire for truth, the Binaries called for the day when worms were buried in mud and holes were filled with lies and treason. Too late, too late for them as I watched with stimulating jubilation when the last Binary faded into the funked, leathery innards of oblivion.

Yellow Hands

From the darkest, most fucked up corners of my brain, yellow hands, as if born from syrupy innards where old stars collapsed under their own bodies, pulled me towards that indescribable darkness. A bizarre grunt, strangely alluring, throbbed and heaved with the orgasmic rhythm like some hulking beast slung atop a mountain peak.

Thoughts, so murky but tickled with radiant peculiarity, soon spilled over the banks in my head. Bedsheets transformed into milky pools of starlight as if the untraveled, tenebrous corridors of tomorrow were so easily explored when suddenly, golden fingers pressed my body underneath the cream-like waters.

Breathing didn't matter to me, but the sensation, in and out, catastrophized to the point of cold ecstasy—cradled within the palms of wild, unadulterated pleasure did I yearn for yellow hands to drag me beneath a bed of stars.

Dragons
and Closets

Closets were caves;
beware the toxic dragons
disguised as men.

The Third Triangle

Scales, skins, and overgrown expectations at the edges of crooked bedrooms and demented closets where I found myself entrapped by the claws of toxic dragons. Nothing made sense here, only the flapping of wings and tattered bedsheets like the flags of surrender o'er the bloody fields of conquered armies. Deeper and deeper, I wandered into the place of shattered expectations, chuckles and lugubrious songs chimed in my ears like the rusty clangs of barbells and bones through a dingy, murky locker where I'd wait. A haunting viridescence glowed in every corner, as something unnatural found its way into the world.

Here, no more triangles, or promises, but scales, skins, and overgrown expectations at the edges of crooked bedrooms and demented closets where I found myself entrapped by the claws of toxic dragons.

Self-Internalized

Closets, gym bags, presumed dominance
Wrapped in warped flaws of falsified expectations
And perfumed, manufactured fuckery.
There were no pantheons here, for gods to dwell,
Only men, formed from clay and lies,
who breathed the air of self-hatred
And dehumanized, monstrous realities.

Closets were no different to them,
Though they became deathful cloisters,
Happily, welcomed by self-proclaimed Bro-Gods
who languished in the funk and foulness
That was their own indecision,
Prepared to watch as sneaker and shadow
blot out the last chance they had at happiness.

Adam the Tyrant (You Could Do Better)

You could do better,
he blasted; hands pressed against my face,
flesh judgments strong, but cruel

You could do better;
Smells of toothpaste and beer
filled my nostrils
As he turned me over, my body like meat

You could do better;
Bruises, blood, and flesh spectrums
Painted my body like some unholy insecure canvas
Like it was a game, a silly, fucked up game

You could do better,,
Friends, family, and strangers warned,
Too late though, when angry hands
Found me, my throat, my ribs

You could do better,
I told myself,
Too scared to leave, to run away from the tyrant
Who knew everything as if the stars too,
Were afraid of his wrath

You could do better;
When there was no difference between
Laughter and tears,
And myself began to fade into him

You could do better;
Choices were no longer my own,
the dark machinations of his sinister lust,
Thinly veiled hallucinations of love

You could do better;
Too late were my dark compunctions
and tyrants must fall

You could do better;
I realized when blood, lust, and flesh
Became my erotic nightmare and I knew then,
Tyrants must fall.
You could do better.

Josh the Dragon

Splayed across thighs of gold and flesh, I felt the awful grip of calloused fingers press hard, without concern or caution over my fragile skull. These were the dragons who knew nothing of joys, of satisfactions, only the senseless, mechanical urges to beat, reuse, and toss aside the bodies of lovers, naïve travelers, and the fair-skinned twink-knights who dared think they could tame the dragon. No one could, not even me.

No matter how hard I resisted, it was both untenable and wonderful between muscled canyons, where reason melted away dispelling every terrible desire imaginable, and only the winged monster of dreadful, unfulfilled lust lay before me. The dragon, the man, undiscernible to my eyes, continued an onslaught to my senses, his cachinnations roiling within the deep-purpled-skies, amused by my self-destruction while the calloused fingers pressed even harder the next time, over my broken skull.

Jon the Titan

Crafted in the blood and false expectations of cruel, pragmatic aesthetics, I found myself chained to the foot of some vascular, Promethean thing who wandered the sweat and musk-ridden fields of a hypermasculine hellscape. Barbell-demons, muscle-dragons, and crimson-faced Bro-Gods wallowed within his shadow as if to gain favor from the monstrous, Herculean sized beast. My love buckled beneath the unholy weight of his blood-filled fingers, hungry for the next piece of plastic protein while truth remained locked inside the garbage pantheons he called his palace.

Jon lumbered across the world, pulling others beneath him with his inane zombified, sexual urges. Too late had I become trapped, realizing there was nothing on the other side, but a creature lost in pathetic self-worth and maniacal worship. I'd break my chains one day and escape the trivialities of his dark kingdom.

Frank the Imposter

I dream of him,
>Or were they nightmares?

Truths never mean to be
>Realized, standing over

Me while thick hands
>Told me everything'd be okay,

Alright but really wasn't,
>Everything was alright

He's only in a mood,
>Passing soon like thunderstorms

Struck me
>Over and over,

He held me every time
>Over and over,

When the mood struck
>Me as if lightning

Felled an ancient oak tree
>Ready to die,

Standing for a thousand years
>Craving a scorched piece of love,

He laughed, he struck
>Never in the same place twice,

Always so gentle though
        Ready to fall like those oak trees,

To dream of him no more,
        Or was *he* my nightmare?

Jesse Star-Eater

He ate everything, licking the crumbs of stars from his fingers, a god whose hunger was never satisfied, as he lounged atop a pile of bones. Behind a rocky, well-shaped countenance, the truth formed by grotesque thirsts and deranged appetites throbbed within the body of the old colossus.

He smiled, gaze so familiar though terrifying some nights, down at what remained of me, prepared to consume the remnant bits of my life, a shadowy crumb between saliva-coated nails.

Planets themselves ran towards the blackest nights from the wide hands of the Star-Eater, but no one was safe from his deep, unforgiving hunger. Days grew shorter, as everything was pulled into him; I was pulled into him, towards the girthy, heavy center of his enormity while he continued his feed on existence and without care for the light; he ate everything, including my love.

Bro-Gods and Jock-Queens

Leather solaces and gutted dreams behind suits and jockstraps, the uniforms whereby heteronormativity tightly pulled o'er the mouths of a humbled, submissive yesterday with laughing closet-top-gods and barbell-demons.

Masquerading in muscles and vainglorious shit-talking songs, sweat-operas and gilded palaces, these Promethean children who damned the idealism of difference only to drown in protein-based muck for another brother, helpless through the mirrors, underneath the benches where Jock-Queens hid from flesh-sculpted truths and gutted dreams.

Thrown again inside locker-room-myths where the inevitable cyber-fuckery might keep the monsters at bay, topped and swallowed, they found the gates sealed shut. Fist and face covered in sweat-songs and brand name security blankets, they'd make their tombs in the glorified temples mummified by internalized fear of their own insecure demons.

Sean the Leviathan

Thick and heavy were his thoughts which pulled me down like a monster from the sea. Compelled I was, to drink from the salty oceans provided by his anger and love despite the dread and dumb-belled nightmares which clashed in my mind every night. Every day he grew with vile, manipulative blood-stroked mania as if another ship swallowed through his wide, terrible jaws.

Still, closer I found myself pressed into tight sweats pulled across a grotesque mass where vascular flesh-stars dotted the all too familiar horizon. I was running out of time. *He craves the meat*, those before me said, familiar with the monster, who tried too late to warn. Too late, they were helplessly devoured. Set one, press two until rolled into that ruthless existence, which was Sean.

Drew the Black Hole

Drew closer, and
      deeper inside the inevitability
         that was a black hole
Drew closer,
      Gravity would do the rest...
         Then I'd fall forever, and ever
Drew closer,
      The inward fear like stars dying,
         Collapsed in on themselves
Drew closer,
      Until no light escaped,
         The darkness that pulled me
Drew closer,
      Whispering the terrors of tomorrow,
         Through the shadows of yesterday
Drew closer,
      And closer when
         No time or space mattered,
Drew closer,
      No reason
     Except precarious freefall
         Towards the laughing dark.

IV

Cycles Over Cycles

When enough is enough, it's never
enough until cycles over cycles
repeat enough is enough is enough.

The Fourth Triangle

Every night it was as if the stars in their spectral radiance had prophesied; I saw the twinkling glow of triangles in the night. Those lights terrified me, reminded me of the world I found myself trapped;

Every night I saw the corpse of triangles caught in the amethystine star-web above, struggling to break free as I did the same in places here which confined and hid me;

Every night from my truth without any sign things might change or light across the horizon. Only the dark ambivalence which crept ever so slowly;

Every night with every tug on my mind and my heart, despite the infinite incarceration of stars, I'd break them free, rip the foundations of abusive gods and see triangles in the night.

Brute

Devils, beast, gods, and master,
The names I used to know him;
Hands, my breath, demonic playthings,
The control he had over me.

Every day my world grew smaller,
Devils, beast, gods, and master,
The names I used to know him;
Hands, my breath, his fucked up playthings,
Control was all around me.

Worthless, empty, *help, get out!*
The pleas inside me, screaming,
Every day the world grew smaller,
With names he used to own me.

There's Always Tomorrow, Until There's Not

Always was the promise of another day when I stood in his awful presence, despite his poison kisses and ashen face. Tomorrow felt so close until it wasn't. Pushed further into the night where godless lights and star-bones looked down at me with pity and fear, mostly fear, between the feet of a monster who dwelled in a palace of hate and lies.

Built atop the twink-bodies, millions like me who walked the path of stale colognes, unholy fantasies, and monstrous eroticisms only to cower in lust and dread, beneath his step. Unaware of his true intentions, the vast demented thing lumbered towards me; fingers like pillars of cracked marble slammed with heavy, primal desire against my body. One after the other, and I knew I was too late to flee, when I stood in his awful presence. Throttled by the scent and sanguinity of his madness, knowing there's always tomorrow, until there's not.

I Swore by the Stars

The stars and their sin, locked in vaults of pus and shame, combined with treasures like tortuous, shiny reminders that nothing would ever be the same;

The stars inside broken closets, flicking like cheap lights, bulbs that revealed my regret as I walked the path of unspeakable acts where desire bled into obligation;

The stars were his trash-whores, his playthings he'd seldom wished upon inside those caskets and closets;

The stars I swore by the false promises he made, lines and scars, palms that piled atop my frail body while I cried over and over;

The stars weren't enough! We aren't enough, but little drops of dust and skin collected beneath nails and nothingness like baneful idiosyncrasies;

The stars died, when there was nothing left, but the shell of what I once was locked inside a vault of pus and shame.

A Bundle of Sticks

Inside a terminal of stars, I found myself clutched against broad arms, displaced and othered, sired under the guise of disparaging eyes and scornful philosophies, though I was nothing to *them*, but everything to *him*. A pile of sticks, collected from some nameless wood where the little birds gathered on broken trunks, felled without a second thought by people who didn't give a fuck about me, or him, or those like us. We were brought inside this terminal of dead stars, the ones left behind from a forest culled down in the wake of progress. Uncertain futures erected, if not merely for the sake of themselves, to cast doubt over the present and burn the world we knew to the ground. It was like we were nothing but a useless pile of sticks.

Piles and piles of them, queer-shaped trunks, twinkish bodies, brought to some mutilated nexus-point, where the judgement cast, and hammers fell over sword and soul. Faceless executioners with rusty axes cared not for my fate. Holding me close as we waited our turn, he was still there, as we wandered through the jagged pragmatisms of this white no-place, where neutron stars and bad dreams kindled sparks of awful truths at our feet. Treacherous, ivory goblins danced while we were burned alive inside a terminal of stars, where I found myself clutched against broad arms, displaced and othered, sired by the guise of disparaging eyes and scornful philosophies, though I was nothing to *them*, but everything to *him*.

Masc (4) Masc

Put me on a pedestal, take me off the box, only to live on someone else's rock. How long can I live inside a sheath of armor, protected inside myself, straight-acting for the sake of no one or myself, consumed within the star-riddled dread of *never-good-enough* or *someday-maybe*, when I'll catch the eyes of the colossus who'll never see the twink-things or femme-boys who scurry below him tearing themselves to pieces for a swipe of attention from someone who could care less?

We live our lives online, inside the pedestal, transforming ourselves, destroying ourselves to worship the Bro-Gods and Binary Masters who presume themselves the bizarre taskmasters of our fantasies. Contorting our own images, what else was there to do, but to detach from the nightmare? Throw ourselves off the pedestal?

I can't do this anymore...

Star Boned, Washed Up

Deep inside the wide, tenebrous voids above, I saw the bones of what used-to-be, the paint which covered the canvas of night. The empty wastes where I played with gods in sickened pantheons and palaces of flesh and dream, when without cause or care they left me inside out, twisted and used like the stars themselves.

Lights with no purpose, but to flicker until bleak heat-death or find the next cycle to drain, derive, then blast their star-stuff across the already stretched canvas for pondering eyes to muse o'er the bones of what-used-to-be, the star-boned wastes, forgotten and useless, washed up.

Mythopoeia

The Shepard's bliss was a lie
to be bold, be daring,
and never cry or shed a tear.

Emotions condemn, painting idols
for the man behind the mirror in the closet,
where expectations were like the trophy-hunting predators
who thought themselves
primal sentinels of a false-identity.

Never theirs to begin with,
never *man* enough
to admit reason to fault
or they might as well be machine,
deprived of a soul,
to prize fire over flesh,
the blood of cowards,
Pittance for plastic courage,
and they paid the price.

The Shepard's bliss was a lie
to be bold, be daring,
and never cry or shed a tear,
to always stand at the gates of Valor and Death.

A Promethean Joke

I was, or wasn't
The antithesis of his desire
Unable to transform, transfer
my baggage into a vestige, vesicle,
Reusable fortitude whereupon
I'd be free from his guttural embrace,
Rusty tongues and tatters.

I was, or wasn't
Everything he thought I'd be
But there wasn't much to do
Except lay me at the feet
Of a monster whose creation
Wasn't my responsibility;
High flesh, and unscalable peaks
Of emotionless, cold indifference
Touched me as if he held everything,
Even the stars, even my soul of clay
This Promethean curse or joke. Simply

To proclaim I was, or wasn't
Everything, but the stars.

His Palace of Apathy

You don't care enough, he screamed through jagged half-smiles caught on the sheets of cold manipulations underneath what-should-be, fallen off supple, gray lips. Truth bled with lies behind tall doors of crumbling granite and gaudiness; a house of self-destructive, pressured seductions became my prison. Coiled in by beliefs of his delusions, dogma, and spoon-fed phlegm, there was only dis-interested paresthesia which poured over my frail body like some sweet, once in a lifetime treat. *Better, but I wish you'd try harder*, he'd sigh rolling over on the regretful bedsprings, speaking out both sides of his mouth.

Cosmic Orgasms

I craved
the endless,
the overwhelming,
cosmic yearning...

The Fifth Triangle

Unrequited, unrelinquished, unending,
Three promises made to the stars'
Infinite, overwhelming mass;
A love without end.

Ever expanding, the shapeless
growth of the universe
Unimaginable and great;
A lust without reason.

Primal urges, seductive
Pulling towards the center
Unrequited, unrelinquished, unending;
My love without end.

Oblivion's Bedroom

There were no words to describe the pain, cocooned by hallucinations of cosmic pleasure while wrapped in the bosom of Oblivion's shapelessness. Pectorals of light where sublime, bizarre shapes danced across my eyes, threw my body at speeds which ripped apart the densest stars; if I wasn't already doomed, it didn't matter; the needle-like euphoria which emblazoned what was left of my perceived sense beautified my decayed conscious, as I saw star-death and dreams curdle beneath the hands of a god, and I was their willing plaything. There were no words, but sweet comfort, inside Oblivion's bedroom.

My Nameless, Empty Lust

When the Palaces of Oblivion were crumpled into ash and memory, I was left with the desperate taste of what-if lingering on my lips. How I longed for his endless, sweet kiss wrapped in the majesty of entropy, but strung through theoretical false promises that someday I'd see him again, held beneath those pectoral star-mounds where planet, pulsar, and black holes compressed into something unexplainable by the weight of his beauty.

Reduced to neurons, my colossus of dreams lumbered across spacetime where I was forever doomed to wonder if I'd ever know the pleasure of imagination again, when the Palaces of Oblivion were rebuilt; I'd embrace the Rainbow Gods once more.

At The Edge

In the beginning, I was told there were no stars, but only milky drops of existence which bathed the wonder and want of the Voids. Soon the spiral arms of the galaxy begged me, only with gentle longing at first, but the dark yearning of that vast thing was all that mattered in the end.

Towards the protrusion of infinity, burgeoning with size, depressed beneath my heavy, ancient desires, the scars of history were revealed to the eyes of existence.

Floods of pain, pleasure, and heat ripped at my lonely center of mass until I collapsed in entirety onto the Void in a breathless, sustained relief. In the end, stars, planets, and even galaxies fell from me where I screamed, bemused by cosmic release.

I Crave Infinity

Nothing could stop me from insatiable drumbeats of thirst which smacked the dry, empty ruins behind my timid eyes. Still, I had to quench the longing, to find some way to hold that treasure where even gods transformed into corpses in their struggle to combat my craven hunger.

I craved more, while my loins were wracked with heat and pain, while the stars in higher towers were tucked safely behind Saturn's cradle, wrestled my growing terror;

I craved more space, more voids to which my needs could be met though never achieved until washed away in the white-hot fantasies of what-if and someday-soon;

I craved more gods, beasts, and nameless, worthless symbols floating in darksome webs of the night to fill my raw, ancient, needs;

I craved more reason to live for the possibility that the stars might fall into my lips, through my heart, ripped into atom and aroma only for me to dance in jubilation to have swallowed a crumb of infinity;

I craved more, piece by piece until even the coldest fractures of existence weren't enough, and enough was never enough, and the last ruins behind my timid eyes stopped me from insatiable drumbeats of thirst;

Gods, I craved more, to embrace infinity and hold him until he collapsed in my arms, crushed by the endless weight of my lust-drenched desire, and there wasn't anyone who'd keep me from him...

I craved infinity.

The Pleasure of Rainbow Gods

I pressed against the night, the underbelly of the gods where through those scar-tissued lights, I saw the twilight bleed new stars and galactic secrets, harder and harder until the muscle of the purpled belly recoiled at my touch. Through the vast unimaginable wastes, I traveled to find the great ones whose skin sparkled like amethyst with a Dionysian thirst where they'd bathe the stars in glowing spectral dust.

Gray lips and tube-machines spilled onto my cheeks where I saw the silvery visage of spectral gods, painted in every color, concept, and grace. Down they came from amethystine castles which hung in the night as if to fool the stars there were other lights more beautiful and precious than they, these Rainbow Gods swayed in the purpled darkness with wrathful lust. Cybertronic eyes found me, beheld with the intensity of a billion wanton cruelties; these were not gods bound to oaths of blood and song, but Dionysian realties built with metal, ribbons, and bone.

Across pointed towers and bizarre cityscapes, I found the edge of existence on a chasm where oceans of white light whirlpooled below me in a cacophonous, dreadful, and exhilarating typhoon of rapturous, orgasmic fury. I pressed against the night, until o'er the event horizon, I was swallowed into the tenebrous webs of nameless space only to writhe in endless, terrible desire beneath the underbellies of gods.

Size Queen

Possibilities were endless,
      in the thick, purple night;
I had to have him,
      Everything from stars to song
Exhausted with nameless ecstasy,
      Nothing was enough
He wasn't enough,
      Beneath the bedsheets of stars
Burning, writhing, dreaming,
      Cycles begin again
Bodies seized in entropy
      Soon lost in scale,
Wishing, dreaming for more,
      Hoping, thinking he was more
Revelations, destructions,
      Cycles begin anew
And I'd have him, again
      In the thick, purple night,
Endless possibilities,
      Though, he'd never be enough.

Spaghettification

Brain-scars and collapsible dream-bodies penetrated the heavy,
unyielding dark, as I was pulled into some stringy, visceral
mass towards a hungering pit. Ruptured and torn, I felt my star-
boned cries echoed throughout the webs of night where even the
fire-orbs cowered, and dared to wonder at the immensity of
Gravity's swollen dominance.

No one could've imagined the thrusted lunacies which pushed me
deeper inside that which was undeniably rapturous. Despite the
fear of being lost inside him, I cried jubilantly into the
emptiness with gratuitous song. Never did I dare, or wonder, for
too late was the price of my submission when I crossed the
threshold, compressed into his dream-body.

Colossus of Dreams

He was the colossus of dreams, standing sentinel over my darkest
pleasures and phantasies. Standing endlessly tall, he straddled
the oceans where imagination convened with the fragility that
was reality; my gaze fixed towards his northernmost peak. Salt
air, pine tree, and the freshwater waves which clapped against his
flesh was enough to conjure a feeling of protection, love,
and majesty while he loomed ever-present.

I never climbed towards *his summit*, but wondered at the
possibility one day, when the oceans might rise, or the stars
fall, allowing me the chance to finally reach him.

Bleeding Rainbows

Where old queens, once dressed in neon, gold, and blessed nightmares, cluttered the cities of light and stars; I saw rainbows fall from skies of flesh and silk.

They were the skeletons of us, the burgeoning spectrums throbbing against a glassy horizon, beat after beat, dripping with liquescent, milky stars.

Rainbows like wilted bodies, bowed and broken, naked with truth and wet with stardust continued to shine, despite the heaviness of someday which pulled o'er the infinite skies.

And so, the old queens continued their dances, frolicking through the darkness while I smiled, bleeding with rainbows and light.

Rainbow Gods
and Gray Gardens

There were no gods here...

The Sixth Triangle

There were no Rainbow Gods,
Only rumors like dead flowers in the gardens of history.
Soft remembrances as if the last kiss from a lover,
or old friend to plant the seeds
left behind in this garden one day
to grow again, to sing again,
to flower again in these Gray Gardens.

We're All Bags of Bones

Empty sacks and blood-drenched philosophies were the only promises and awful expectations of Someday. Bones, gods, and twisted gifts I'd seen across the star-glazed night where names meant nothing, but bones were everything in the end. Bodies, bruises, and barren dreams, bereft of imagination, stripped entirely of the blazing conflagrations as if infesting my consciousness.

I'm left in the endless depths of silence at the bottom of a hospital bed in the city of nowhere, emblazoned with scars and ribbons as if to mark my corpse and carrion dreams. The last of a numbered few, a triangle, a tattoo, an empty sack because bones were everything in the end.

Where His Gray Lips Were Mine

Tube-machines and flesh-buttons covered his skin, while his body
became slave to a new universe of metal coordination and plastic
gods. Still, through his universe, he was the same, despite the
gray lips which met mine, and the frail body which sunk into the
swamp of cotton blankets and corporate fabric.

> Supple were his lips,
> > and blind were his eyes,

Covered in heavy cataracts; he was everything even if my smile
was nothing but the gray stars. After every kiss, I felt the
possibilities of a billion galaxies burn and cool, endlessly,
and through the tube-machines and flesh-buttons I prayed,

> He never saw my tears,
> > and blind his eyes remained.

The Milk of Stars

One indifferent shot, wrenched and blasted through the center of existence curdled the fragile cosmogony of light and truth. Beyond the veil of vengeful faces, I felt history unravel with seizing, violent, thunderous voices cackling whereupon the tyranny of expectation ruptured my reasoning, as I gazed upon the face of a hideous, metallic creature. Binary Things composed of choice and charnel visions, they were the culmination of everything that never-was, pressing me and those alike towards the darkest parts of ourselves.

They carried their daggers and dark hearts proudly into the deepest nights, where not the agony of stars could be heard. And it was everything they wanted, despite the impossibility of it all, until the corpse of Progress lay freshly decayed in the streets of Tomorrow, bled entirely with the milk of stars.

Children of the Plague

Condemned for something we can't control, wrapped in symbols meant to downplay, to placate, to manipulate death inside waiting rooms turned into false-memorials and phony-graves without well-wishes forgone for the dead rainbows, but silent and forgotten were the prayers when monitors stopped, ribbons raised like flags, and cream-guilt reconciled while more bodies filled yet another room.

No one brought us flowers, sung anthems, or chorused parades, but only wretched pomp disguised by the Creatures too culpable to admit their fault in a system responsible for the consumption of stars. The lights which ignited a thousand generations, dimmed for a single moment, left us to wander in the darkness, the children of a plague that was never ours.

Stonewalled (Sing for Myself)

Cancers, quarantines, and plagues
Followed us relentlessly throughout the ages;
We were the descendants of rainbows,
Colored in the light of tomorrow,
Threatened by ugly faces and laughing gods
Who called for the bodies of rainbows,
Stained with the blood of tomorrow
Over and over until we believed closets were our home.

Fortresses built with lies and false expectations,
Despite the dark umbrage of cruel masters,
We held the songs of the universe,
Composed in flesh and star-boned nights,
Until the music grew so loud, everyone heard us,
Sang with us, the songs of tomorrow,
Forbidden by crimson-faced stoics and closeted-neophytes!

Here, confined in the junkyards and alleyways,
Beneath the sun and stars with gray gardens,
Atop the forgotten corpses of rainbows, we made our home
Safe from cancers, quarantines, and plagues,
No longer confined to grim structures, or dank attics;
We were the children of rainbows.

Orion's Path

Along the path through the floor of an ancient wood where bodies of mushrooms, sprigs, and flowers litter the brown duff, a young hunter followed the familiar melodies of beautiful, gray wizards. A path veiled in cautious shadows; he knew the other side was abundant in mythic rewards: *it had to be*. The music continued, hypnotically pulling him towards a place beyond the mountains, where the old sorcerers once sang—

under ageless stars, the galaxy's heart, here the gray wizards rest, here they wait for you

—along the path through the floor of an ancient wood where a young hunter followed the melodies of beautiful, gray wizards.

The Myth of the Gray Garden

Old houses with wilted flowers in the shadow underneath a lazy mountain where the gray garden rested in dreams both black and white as if blasted in cinematic nostalgia. The discoloration and beauty warped behind tired oaks whose leaves managed to hide old tuna cans, tattered furs, and foggy dreams were the unspoken desires of so many who sought to find the garden, tucked away in a place between sleep, sex, and never-again.

I'd never let them find it though, for it was as precious as a lover's first touch, sweet and secretive, but never willing to give up that which cannot be taken by fire or fear. It was my hiding place away from the brutalized reality, tucked under a lazy mountain, the gray garden remained hidden.

The Gray Garden

Carrion perfumes and seductive visions led me towards a great tower which loomed above the alien terrain, riddled with twisted branches, violet blooms, and sparkling lakes of milky light. I believed it to be the end, the other side of an already cruel confinement which held me trapped, pressed in the bleached false promises;

I crossed the edge,
      Into the gray garden,
I crossed the edge,
      Into the graveyard of triangles and truths

Beneath the familiar sight of a thick obelisk, swaying in the night where each step crunched over the moist earth. Soil rich in the mud of atrocity, aromas I never thought I'd smell again compelled my legs closer to the base of the structure, as I stood paralyzed by its murk and majesty;

I crossed the edge,
      Into the gray garden,
I crossed the edge,
      Through the doors of the tower,
I crossed into the gray garden.

The Edge of the Garden

Higher and higher the bile splashes, acidic and happy until soon the closet-stomach was devoured entirely by a heinous, liquescent self-loathing as if impossible to expel through vomit or volition. Closets cursed me, the Queens freed me, and still I was made to believe nothing mattered wrapped in my demented sense of self-worth where hordes of Bro-Gods and Binary-Monsters laughed, *you don't matter.*

I'd pulled these chains once before. Caskets across the wastes of a mouth of mirrors whose lips hungered for the last fleshy bits.

Believed to be nothing but a last resort, I pushed away their calloused fingers and found myself inching towards a garden at the edge of a gray-mattered reality. An asphodel where elysian nightmares were placated by the crumbling pieces of closets and caskets, no longer cursing me.

I'd conquered them at the edge of the garden.

Bleed No More

Lights less signified,
shadows without reason
when Rainbows
have nothing left to give.

The Seventh Triangle

Embrace the dark, together in silence, light, love, and shadow. Three sides of totality denote the trajectory of broken spectrums, no longer shattered pieces of self, but beautiful reflections of possibility as clear as the glittering orbs within the webs of night. Each side, three infinite representations of the latter, continuing onward and forever spinning away from hatred and horror; together, light, love, and shadow embrace the dark.

The Last Rainbow God

Hold me close beneath the glittery, spectral resplendence which burned in that far away somewhere. Clutched against the metallic pectoral embrace, sculpted with remnant pieces from the last Rainbow Gods, I watched while a beautiful decay covered my body and the oxidized skin which spread almost endlessly from marble, muscle, and mitochondrial desires; this broken colossus felled like a tree in the Gardens of Oblivion.

The crown of silence was unbearable when suddenly, the leathery flapping of old wings crashed through the old canyons, their thunderous echoes a warning from the past that there wasn't much time left to enjoy a final embrace for old gods, lost friends, or singing sad songs. Too soon would the shadows and closet-bastards attempt to consume the gardens constructed meant for sanctuary within plumes of fire and death as if dancing to some sycophantic, erotic nightmare.

Hold me close, I pleaded one last time while the neon moon climbed slowly into the night, clutched against the body of a broken colossus, the last Rainbow God.

Somewhere Over the Rainbow

Familiar songs sung through crinkled lips like glass-reflected, darksome melodies played across broken, beautiful spectrums of light. The same old song to some, but Neon-Queens who strutted beneath the disco and dread of forgotten histories kicked up those awful troubles and tumults and case them out, like houses dropped from a dust-devil's stomach.

A song played throughout the generations as if anthems trumpeting where we marched across the yellow-brick-bodies of lovers, laymen, and lepers; no more would the broken glass make us bleed or cackling witches keep us from returning home, so long as we sang familiar songs.

Bleed No More

Rainbows without blood,
Ribbons of bone,
They cried tears from stars,
And bleed no more;

Fragile kisses,
Scarce with love.
Held by closet-bodies
Broken, bent, and burnt to cinder,
But bleed no more;

Fears coated in dragon scales
Muted cycles and green gods,
Who preached false love,
And bleed no more;

Light lost to shadow
And rainbows without blood,
Ribbons, or bone
Never to cry tears from stars
And bleed no more.

Through the Curtain (A Reprise)

Through the doors, or curtain perhaps
When stars have gone to bed,
Dragons asleep in their caves,
The closets in piles to burn,
With not much left to say
I'll take his hand again.

A familiar song, I knew those hands,
Echoes of a terrible past,
Though I wasn't scared anymore,
No evil to dissuade me, for I'd walked the path
Through light and entropy,
I'll take his hand again.

Through the curtain, perhaps a door,
When we've gone to bed,
Rainbow Gods walked the Earth again,
And the closets buried forever,
There's nothing left to say,
I'll take his hand again.

When Rainbows Bleed

When rainbows bleed, the skies
were filled with corpses of light as if
the caskets, now closets were opened
for the universe to see;

When rainbows bleed,
no lights would hide the darkness
which sought to bind them to their
Earthly prisons or flesh-temples;

When rainbows bleed, no one knew
exactly what to expect, but to see the light
for what it really was meant to be,
Prisms misconstrued by Binary Masters, Bro-Gods, and Toxic
Dragons
swallowed in cycles over cycles;

When rainbows bleed, there was only the sweet,
gentle kiss of his lips on mine
after the fall of star-blood and light
o'er the ruined closet-bodies
scattered in every direction;

When rainbows bleed, there were no more Binary Masters,
or barbell temples where
the sacrifice of flesh, mind,
and fucked up fantasy were
played up as if some defiled ritual
to sate those mythologized,
haughty phantoms and their games;

When rainbows bleed, enough was enough
and the game was over.
No more dark jubilations,
but Uranian joy everlasting
when ribbons swayed in the wind no longer
patronizing tatters,
and rainbows bleed no more.

Lights less signified,
    shadows without reason
        when Rainbows
            have nothing left to give.

ABOUT THE AUTHOR

Maxwell I. Gold is a Jewish American multiple award nominated author who writes prose poetry and short stories in cosmic horror and weird fiction with half a decade of writing experience. Three-time Rhysling Award nominee, and two-time Pushcart Award nominee, find him at *www.thewellsoftheweird.com*

ABOUT THE CONTRIBUTORS

Angela Yuriko Smith is a third generation Shimanchu-American and award-winning poet, author, and publisher with 20+ years of experience as a professional writer in nonfiction. Publisher of *Space & Time* magazine (est. 1966), producer of Exercise Your Writes, two-time Bram Stoker Awards® Winner, and HWA Mentor of the Year for 2020, find Angela at *www.angelaysmith.com*

Martini is an erotic illustrator from the Netherlands. Follow him on Twitter at *@Martini_Art_*

Alec Ferrell is a multimedia producer, graphic designer, and musician based in Durham, NC. Check out his print, digital, and audio/video work at *www.clearlymedia.net, @clearlyalec, and @clearlyrecords*

Joshua Viola is a *Denver Post* bestselling author, Colorado Book Award winner, Splatterpunk Award nominee, and the owner of Hex Publishers. Learn more at *www.JoshuaViola.com*

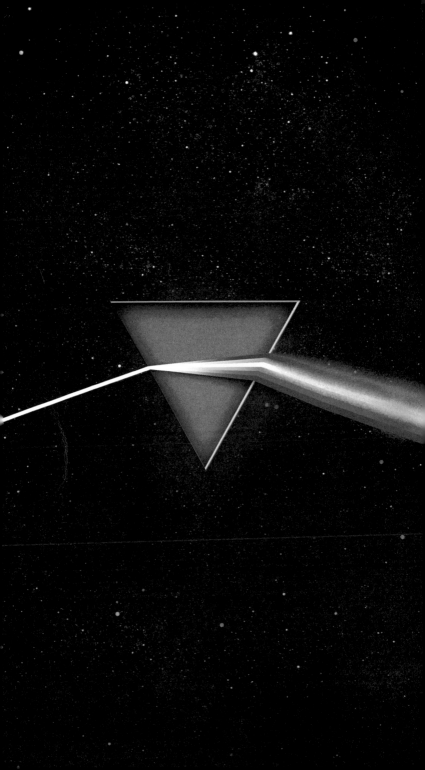

BLEEDING RAINBOWS AND OTHER BROKEN SPECTRUM
is a lurid poetic journey explored through the eyes of the gay sexu
experience. From flesh gods and cyberlust to cosm
orgasms, Pushcart and Rhysling Award-nominee Maxwell I. Gol
takes readers on a surreal expedition across a vast prismat
spectrum of homoeroticism. Over 60 original poems transcend th
tantalizing—and sometimes frightening—realities of a quee
narrative that will leave readers thirsting for more. Interior include
7 original NSFW color illustrations by erotic artist Martini.

"With this bold collection of desiccated erotic fantasies, Maxwell I. Gold
creates a dread-palace of beautiful perversion."
—LEE MURRAY, four-time Bram Stoker Award®-winning author of
Grotesque: Monster Stories

"A bold, visceral collection that pushes past comfort zones into a fever
dream of raw, ugly truths refracted by the spinning disco ball of Gold's
audacious poetic storytelling."
—VINCE A. LIAGUNO, Bram Stoker Award®-winning editor of
Unspeakable Horror: From the Shadows of the Closet

"If Zeus picked up Ganymede in a gay bathhouse, if Laura met Carmilla in a
BDSM dungeon for vampires, their tales of supernatural sexual awakening
would resemble the poetry in Maxwell Gold's terrifying—and incredibly
sexy—*Bleeding Rainbows and Other Spectrums*."
—SUMIKO SAULSON, Bram Stoker Award®-nominated author of
The Rat King, A Book of Dark Poetry

18+

ISBN 978-1-7365964-4-9
90000

9 781736 596449

HexPublishers.com / Printed in the USA / Cover Layout by Damonza and Joshua Viola